CREATE YOUR
F U T U R E !

IDEA-RICH
INNOVATIVE LEADERSHIP

BOB 'IDEA MAN' HOOEY

AUTHOR, WHY DIDN'T I THINK OF THAT?

3rd edition (updated 2024)

Success
Publications

Box 10, Egremont, Alberta, Canada T0A0Z0
www.SuccessPublications.ca

Leadership, creativity and strategic thinking

"Leadership," says Peter Drucker, *"is lifting a person's vision to higher sights, raising a person's performance to a higher standard, and building a personality beyond its normal limitations."*

The foundations of successful, *effective* leadership start with each person taking personal responsibility for their own actions as part of a group, while feeling confident enough to suggest and accept revisions in team goals and performance. The foundations of long-term, profitable growth and success are built on CREATIVE personal and corporate leadership. Someone once said, **"The best way to predict YOUR future is to create it!" Why not lead it!**

You might be asking, *"What does leadership have to do with vision or creativity?"* Quite frankly, everything!

Our customized leadership program, **Prepare Yourself to WIN!** -- is all about honing your skills as a *creative* leader and teaching those skills to your team so they succeed or win. Visit **www.BobHooey.training** or more details and program information on how you can engage the creative mind of Bob 'Idea Man' Hooey to help your team win and *create the future* they want.

To survive and thrive in this global competition, we need to successfully learn new styles of applied problem-solving, and innovation.

We must be willing to take personal leadership in using them in our own activities, and in the creative interaction with our fellow workers, our teams, our suppliers, and our clients.

Consistent use and improvement sharpen your creative leadership skills.

"Management is doing things right; Leadership is doing the right things." **Peter Drucker**

Our goal, as leading edge creative leaders, is *effectively* handling opportunities for growth, as well as problems, challenges, and mistakes. It is being able to cut through to the *root* causes, *mining* deep, and developing real solutions to put into action in conjunction with our various teams. It is also providing solid, *visionary* leadership at the senior level, which inspires those who follow you.

My objective in this book (*as in all my leadership, business and career development publications*) is to assist you in acquiring some new creative leadership skills, problem solving models, and to introduce creativity tools that will help you in your personal life, career, and interaction with your clients, staff, and co-workers. To help you creatively grow your skills and to succeed!

We also include problem-solving processes to creatively outline solutions -- workable solutions -- solutions than can be implemented tomorrow morning. I trust you will discover new approaches to the problems you may encounter.

I challenge you to see them as opportunities to grow and change the way you live, lead, or do business. A wise man told me that; *"My ability to earn would be directly dependent on my ability to solve problems, to help people make decisions."*

In business, particularly, we are paid for our ability to creatively solve our client's problems; by the provision of services or products. As an executive, leader, or new entrepreneur, creativity is our stock in trade. We will succeed as we creatively serve and solve our client and staff needs.

Each of these tools and tips can be applied in at least three directions:

- Problem-solving and decision making
- Strategic planning
- Tapping our inner genius or Creative S.O.U.L.

"Our productivity -- often survival -- does not depend solely on how much effort we expend, but on whether or not the effort we invest is in the right direction." anonymous

The tools we touch on will help you define the direction and outline the process you need to successfully reach the goals you set. To hone your leadership edge, you will need to dig in deeper in their application. They can be used in *birthing* your dreams for new products and services; or in solving perplexing problems for your team members you encounter enroute.

Some objectives and benefits of unleashing your *creative* leadership in your quest to create the future you want in your career or business:

- **More accurate information** - increased productivity by better communication
- **Effective coordination** of activities - how do I fit in the big picture
- **Improving the flow of ideas** - both internally (up and down) and externally
- **Facilitating the decision-making process** - being an agent of change
- **Training** - cross training, uniform training, and to provide an interactive forum
- **Building morale** - encouraging teamwork and mutual support

Occasionally, we need to pause and gain a higher perspective, to make sure we are still heading in the right direction. Our efficiency can be misdirected if we are not going where we want in pursuit of our goals.

One of the biggest lessons I've learned about creative problem solving; **there is always a solution;** frequently, there are **a multitude of solutions.** If your problem is industry specific, you might want to talk to others in your industry and **"Thunder-think"** some answers, or bring it to your next Chamber of Commerce or trade or professional association meeting.

The other lesson: **I'm not the only one with a problem.**

Sharing a problem can lead to solving it. Someone not directly involved in your problem may see a solution or thread that unravels it, due to the difference in his or her perspective or experience. They can see it with objectivity, and perhaps even more clarity, because they are not emotionally involved!

I've written this guide specifically to provide you with tips, techniques, and creative problem-solving models that work in the real world.

I believe passionately in the information presented, and enjoy the opportunity to pass it on. I'd love to share my **Ideas At Work!** with you, and indirectly with your team members. I trust you find it valuable.

I want to see you and your team succeed, and will do whatever I can to facilitate that process. I want to see you use this information in your dealings with each other, and in serving the needs your teams and clients. My longer training programs allow me to coach, confront, and confirm, as necessary to keep your creativity flowing and keep us on track.

Perhaps we can revisit this topic as an on-site program, with the creative involvement of your teams, and spend more time going through it together?

Bob 'Idea Man' Hooey
www.ideaman.net
www.BobHooey.training

Table of Contents

Unlock your 'Creative Leadership' potential

"Ideas are the beginning point of all fortunes."
Napoleon Hill

Growing your career or business to the next level is a worthy goal. Unlocking your 'Creative Leadership' potential draws from the same creative well that allows you to dream and dare and continue to declare to the world*, "I will make a difference!"*

In the time, we share here, I will attempt to kick-start your creativity and challenge your business/ executive *'mindsets'*, to help you look at what you do from a fresh perspective. To expose your senses to the opportunities which surround you; I've created this guide to give you solid ideas in pursuit of that creative leadership quest.

To expand and **Unlock Your 'Creative Leadership' Potential,** explore a few ideas:
- Learn to tap into your **Creative S.O.U.L.: S**eeker of wisdom; **O**penness to people and ideas; **U**nlimited energy; and a high **L**evel of risk and adventure.
- Learn and apply the creative process to your situation: **Preparation, incubation, illumination, and implementation**, or action on the creative thoughts.
- Believe in your creative abilities*. Belief precedes creation!*
- Don't be afraid to ask *'stupid'* questions. There aren't any!

- Challenge your assumptions and existing mindsets. Destroy the old and create the new.
- Give your ideas breathing space to germinate and grow. Nurture them carefully.
- Read outside your normal zone to expand your mind. *(Try some of my books! – Smile! Visit: SuccessPublications.ca)*
- Recruit a creative, collaborative circle of friends and fellow seekers. *(Use a success team)*
- Travel and be open to explore and expand by truly seeing new ideas.
- Learn to explore the web. Visit: www.ideaman.net
- Make a conscientious effort to capture, record, and save your ideas. *(An Idea Journal)*
- See your **Ideas At Work** by using the **Patience** to see it through!
- Remember to have fun! We learn best in times of enjoyment.
- Use "**Thunder-thinking**" (brainstorming to some) to get thinking outside your box.
- Create a special place that sparks and supports your creativity.
- Share and expect synchronicity with the world. Often you get what you expect!
- Encourage idea volume generation with all your connections and teammates.

Just a few thoughts that might help you crank up the volume and burst your locked in 'business' bubble, access your creativity and start applying innovation to your operations.

Creativity is 99% perspiration and 1% inspiration *(Who said it was going to be easy?)*

Bryan Mattimore's excellent creativity book, "99% perspiration" should be in your personal success or organization's library. It should be signed out and being *worn out* by your team.

Our ongoing success and survival in business is directly dependent on our creative ability to profitably solve the problems in our client's lives and operations. We use our innovative solutions to help make their lives and businesses better.

Accessing or tapping into our creativity can be hard work unless you systemize your approach to leadership in your endeavours.

We hear stories of the **'ah-ha' moments** in history, business, and science. These *'lightning bolt'* occurrences nominally come about after many hours of research and applied study into a topic.

I know that is how it usually works in my writing and program creation activities. I research, read my brains out, and take copious notes, before I start writing. They sometimes are *mined* from lessons drawn from past failures.

Consider **Thomas Edison** and the 1000's of attempts to find a sustainable material for the filament for a light bulb.

Take the time to conduct systematic and well-rounded research, coupled with *mining* the lessons learned from your errors and mistakes (and those who you research). This will help fill your mind with the *raw* materials necessary for creative process development.

This is, as you guessed, the *perspiration* part of the creative process and takes an investment on your part.

During the *incubation* period, let your subconscious mind chew on all this material and let it forge new connections with the seemingly unrelated bits of information. Your subconscious will then send these vague feelings or intuitions to the surface or conscious mind. The creative person knows to capture these thoughts, however vague, impractical or wild, for later evaluation and analysis.

Be open and accessible to all ideas – regardless of size

I've seen many people fall to the trap of waiting for the *big idea* – a completely novel idea for a product, project, or service. They sit and wait for sudden inspiration or brilliant flashes of insight. Focusing on big ideas, we can easily become blinded from seeing smaller, otherwise *good* and *valuable* solutions.

Like the story, I heard of an employee in the mailroom who noticed several packages being couriered to the same address. He checked into it and compiled them into one package with instructions on distribution at the receiving end.

His small change in process saved his company tens of thousands of dollars each year.

While not as flashy or showy, these smaller insights and ideas often represent very workable and profitable options. Some can even lay the foundation for other great ideas. Encourage your team to capture or share their ideas with you, and investigate all the options contained.

Consider that the original idea for the $1 billion dollar a year, Levi Strauss Dockers line came from one of their employees - (*a dock worker* ☺) in Argentina.

Time to sweat – perspiration activities

What can you do to fertilize your mind for enhanced brainstorming, or thunder thinking, as I like to call it? **(Thunder thinking – when lightning strikes!)** What kind of research or mental preparation or *perspiration* activities will help you and your fellow leaders and staff?

Successful suggestions that worked for other *creative* thinkers:

- Visit authoritative web sites and learn to use search engines to conduct on-line research
- Constantly revisit and challenge your existing assumptions and mindsets. No sacred cows!
- Remember to have fun! We learn best during times of enjoyment.

- Use Google's news alert program to keep you informed on selected areas (other search engines and web based programs will provide this type of material often daily.) I have several news topics on leadership, creativity and innovation and get emails with links to those stories daily. **Primes my pump!**
- Read books and magazine articles on the issue of topic you are studying or researching. A copy of **'Why Didn't I THINK of That?'** might be a good addition to your library. We provide a good selection of creative leadership, business and career development publications at our website (www.SuccessPublications.ca)
- Map out the information you need, and potential sources where you might find it. Ask open-ended questions to draw out or elicit the most usable and rich information.
- Ask carefully crafted questions of experts in your study. They will often be able to *'kick start'* your creativity, and give you a head up that will advance your process to the next level.
- Don't be afraid to ask seemingly stupid questions – there aren't any!
- Learn to apply the creative four-step process to fully explore your ideas: preparation, incubation, illumination and of course implementation, or acting on the idea.

The 21st Century version of the Three R's

Most creative breakthroughs or innovations are not entirely new. Many *new items* represent creative combinations, adaptations, or modifications of existing services, products, technologies, or materials. Not re-inventing the wheel each time, but taking it a step up in the development of its use and scope.

Fortunately, faster computers, word processing, visual outlining, or diagramming programs make it easier to gather, analyze, and manipulate information fragments into new combinations or versions for use.

This is an amazing time to live and let your creativity flow! This allows you to apply **the 3 R's in your creative process**.

- **Research**, retrieve, and record information.
- **Review** and revise the information you gather.
- **Recombine** or re-use ideas – make new associations between the idea fragments of information you've gathered.

A few concluding thoughts…

With the proper preparation, any of your team members can experience *ah-ha* moments. Properly applied, **each team member can accomplish it.** It takes training, but it is not something only an Einstein would be able to do.

Some final **tips to help facilitate this creative process:**

- **Know where to look** for information. Love learning – become a sponge for information on your topic or field of study.

- **Develop the skills** for asking incisive, well thought-out, open-ended questions that draw out the information, the insights, and the wisdom of those you approach.

- **Experiment with mind mapping** or other right brain stimulation tools to map out your assumptions, questions, insights, concerns, and needs for more information.

- During the interim between your 'Thunder-thinking' or brain-storming sessions, **remain open for additional, *unexpected* insights.**

- Be a creative *sponge* starting with your industry or profession and flowing outward into cross-functional disciplines, business, social or other areas.

- The insight you seek may not be found in the place you live or work, but it is out there. **Cultivate an 'insight-outlook'.** Be open to consider information, insights, trends, and other data mined from multiple perspectives and personal experience.

- Work to identify and understand the inferences, underlying trends, or connections they may contain, and how they might pertain or impact what you are working on in your study.

Food for thought - fuel your creativity

"An idea is a feat of association." Robert Frost

One of the activities used to keep myself fresh and creative is to allow myself to 'free flow' with ideas.

Often *profitable*, creative nuggets will come from spending time *re-thinking* things from a fresh or different perspective.

Allow your mind to wrap around a few of these new thoughts.

Unlock your creativity - let your mind soar! As I've been reminded, **"The best way to predict the future is to create it!"**

You need to fuel the creative part of your brain… to prime the pump. Taking time to reflect on these quotes and thoughts and to creatively engage in the challenge outlined in each of these activities will engage and hone your creative skills. Creativity is a skill, enhanced and enjoyed with increased use.

Remember, *"Imagination is more important than knowledge,"* as **Albert Einstein** taught.

"When the only tool you have is a hammer, you tend to treat everything as if it were a nail."
Abraham Maslow

The most innovating ideas often started with *seemingly* ridiculous thoughts. In fact, the more ridiculous, unusual, or abstract the idea; the more likelihood of it containing the *seed* of a remarkably innovative solution to your problem.

Warm up your creativity. Just for fun, take two *unrelated* objects and imagine as many comparisons or connections between them as possible. For example: an elephant and a diamond. Both have different facets, both come in different sizes and colors, both come from Africa.

Practice mental pinball to build your associative skills. Strong creative thinkers let their thoughts skip, jump, and dart like the activity in a pinball machine. They let their thoughts bounce off ideas and take quantum leaps in a multitude of directions. Take one word or thought and see if you can freely associate 20 items or thoughts. Reach 20… stretch your mind and go for 30.

Creativity in looking at other areas, worlds or industries can spark the solution you need. For example, to create customer loyalty or increased usage you might look at what the airlines are doing with frequent flier miles. Ask yourself what can I do, like the frequent flyer programs, to increase usage in my business? The ideas might just amaze you and be simple to implement.

Do you have a **creative environment** that brings out your best thinking? Create environments that are conducive to creative thought; for example, casual clothes, warm room (not too warm), soft couch, fireplace, soft music, walking outdoors on a lovely day, working is a darkened room, etc.

Just like athletes who go through personal rituals to help themselves psychologically feel and play better; you can create one that works for you. Give this some thought and then **act on it.**

What would a famous person do? Challenge yourself to think how several distinctly different celebrities or historical figures might approach your problem. How would the Pope, John Kennedy, and comedian Jay Leno tackle our problem? What would a Sam Walton do?

Use the ***trigger points*** generated by what you think they would do, as the tools to find the ideas to creatively help you solve your leadership or management challenges.

TEAM THINK: Meet weekly with a 3 to 5-person team for the specific focus of brainstorming solutions to each other's problems. Change at least one person on the team periodically, to help keep the perspectives fresh, the creative energy levels high, and the ideas flowing.

Think Positive - if you want to think creative. Idea killers like, "We've tried that before…" or "That's a dumb idea!" will damper the creative juices and flow quicker than water on the creative flame.

Why not ask yourself, *"How can we build or improve on that?"* or *"Let's look at the workable parts of that idea and see where it will lead us?"* Your perspective can be the *key* that successfully unlocks any problem. *(See how to handle the dream killers in your life on page 77)*

Go for quantity if you want quality. Generate as many ideas as possible - good ones, bad ones, fuzzy ones, even stupid ones - to find the high pay-off, pay-back or usable ones. Just like you would take a multitude of photographs to get enough shots to be able to pick a good one; why not do the same with your idea machines (brains).

Solutions come when least expected - and when they are not forced. While ideas come like love at first sight, those gushers are the exceptions. Trying to *force* an idea is like trying to force love between two people. It usually gives the same results ☺. Ideas come in the shower, while walking, and while day-dreaming.

Team works: Trying to solve a tough problem by yourself can be very stressful. Thunder-thinking, master-minding, or brainstorming with your friends or colleagues can help you get more done in less time - with a better quality of results. It can also be more fun and mutually profitable.

Play to keep your creativity alive. Spend time playing with children - yours or borrowed ones. Being with childlike people is a good way to access the playful part of yourself. This spontaneous part of you is very important to the creative process.

Being willing to explore with childlike abandon and adventure is the secret to the creative process. Give children a set of blocks and they create whole worlds without concern for what we might think; cities, forts, houses, castles, boats, etc. What have you done lately to keep your *inner child* healthy and happy?

Information, time and the ability to solve problems creatively are the most valued currencies in business today.

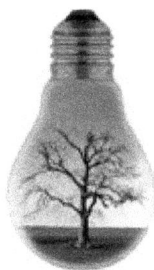

We are learning to use technology (like the Internet) to access information quickly. How do we learn to access creative thinking? Attend a seminar (like one of mine www.ideaman.net); listen to a CD/tape/podcast, read a book, (www.SuccessPublications.ca) buy some of the new creative thinking software like Idea-Fisher, and play. Any one of these will help you raise your Creative IQ and help protect and increase your business and career.

Creatively invest in your future! After all, it is where you will spend the rest of your life! Creatively invest in your leadership future for the same reason!

Laugh a lot, and have fun. Recently I read that we've lost the sense of laughter. Evidently, we now only laugh 6 minutes per day on the average compared to 18 minutes per day average just 20 years ago,

Humor is a good form of relaxation and brain stimulation.

While in this frame of mind we generate more ideas and better ideas. Use fun stuff in-group sessions to facilitate creativity and laugher, e.g. crayons for note taking, candy, or funny prizes for silly and bizarre ideas. Have fun and generate more ideas.

Play the "W*hat if*" game to jump-start your creativity. Change your perspective or basis of looking at the idea or problem at hand.

Ask yourself...

- What can I add?
- Shrink?
- Expand?
- Take away?
- Adapt?
- Modify?
- Substitute?
- Reverse?
- Put to another use?

You might just be pleasantly surprised at the answers to your questions.

Being wrong is part of the creative process.
Creativity in problem solving will lead you down many paths, some of which are dead ends. But being wrong is only a part of the process until you reach a solution. You only have to be right once, and that's the one that counts.

The mistakes, wrongs, and dead ends, are only '*stepping-stones*' to your eventual success. (See page 42 for more ideas on this.)

Stressed out -- not feeling creative? **Take a fun break and visit a toy store.** Play with the toys or at least watch the children doing so. It will help the stress melt away and recharge your brain.

Get past the fear of looking stupid to the risk of success in accessing and acting on your creativity. Our biggest roadblock to creativity is often our fear of looking stupid, appearing different, or looking out of place or silly. Most of this goes back to the '*roots*' of experience as kids and seeing or experiencing how kids who were different were viewed and treated. Kids who were nerds or weirdoes…. but just ask Bill Gates if that matters now?

Believe in YOU as a creative source. Many people do not believe they are creative. You may never be a Michael Jordan, a Tom Hanks, or an Elton John - but you can still act and play and enjoy life in those areas.

You don't have to be an Einstein or Michelangelo to be a strong *creative thinker* and generate ideas to act on in your life and business.

Don't let the negative get to you. Remember the majority has historically been wrong.

Progress and achievement have come, for the most part, from people who were willing to go their own way, to be wrong in the world's eyes in the pursuit of their dreams. Back in the mid-40's the CEO of 20th Century Fox thought people would soon tire of staring at the box we call TV.

Be brave enough to live creatively.

"The creative is the place where no one else has ever been. You must leave the city of your comfort and go into the wilderness of your intuition. You can't get there by bus, only by hard work, risking, and by not quite knowing what you're doing. What you'll discover will be wonderful: Yourself!" Alan Alda

Tackle your fears to unleash your creativity. Society itself, traditions, and self-imposed limitations can build barriers.

Fears can severely hinder the cultivation of creativity:
- fear of making mistakes;
- fear of being seen as a fool;
- fear of being alone;
- fear of being misused;
- fear of losing the love of the group;
- fear of losing the security of habit;
- fear of being criticized;
- fear of being an individual;
- fear of disturbing tradition or going against prevailing thought.

"When you get a grip on the fear that is holding you back, you will see your creativity soar."
Bob 'Idea Man' Hooey

A bit more food for thought to savor

"All things are created twice: first mentally; then physically. The key to creativity is to begin with the end in mind, with a vision and a blueprint of the desired result." Stephen R. Covey

"I submit that creativity will never be a science -- in fact, much of it will always remain a mystery, as much of a mystery as 'what makes the heart tick?' At the same time, I submit that creative is an art - an applied art, a workable art, a learnable art - an art in which all of us can make ourselves more and more proficient, if we will." **Alex Osborn**

"Creativity is especially expressed in the ability to make connections, to make associations, to turn things around and express them in a new way." **Tim Hansen**

You know you're an old dog when you stop learning new tricks. Be teachable to be creative!

"Creativity is the natural extension of our enthusiasm." **Earl Nightingale**

"Creativity involves taking what you have, where you are, and getting the most out of it." **Carl Mays**

"Creativity is like a muscle - it has to be stretched and exercised regularly to keep it fit and functioning." **Gloria Hoffman and Pauline Graivier**

"The creative person is the master rather than the slave of his imagination." **Michael LeBoeuf, Ph.D**

"One of the major factors which differentials creative people from lesser creative people is that creative people pay attention to their small ideas." **Roger von Oech**

$$E = mc^2$$

Creative tips from our friend, Professor Einstein:

- Think things out fresh... be unconventional
- Destroy the old, then create the new
- Tap your imagination
- Consider new ideas, ask new questions, raise new possibilities

Innovate or evaporate
The time to act is NOW!

When would be the best time to start some serious work on innovation in your organization? "Now!" is the short answer.

The gap between imagination and achievement or actualization has never been shorter.

Beginning *somewhere* is always preferable to waiting while your team weighs the options, or while the organization goes bust, or gets left in the dust by those competitors who '*are*' being innovative and creative in this volatile market.

Author of "Leading the Revolution," Gary Hamel advocates that *"radical innovation is the competitive advantage of the new millennium."*

With the aftermath since 911, the Enron fallout, and a general shake up in our economy; a wakeup call is in order. The innovative process can be a challenge to productive change with some organizations' mental constraints and traditionalistic *stuck-in-the-mud* mindsets.

J.K. Galbraith, noted economist once shared, *"Faced with the choice of changing one's mind and proving there is no need to – almost everyone gets busy on the proof."*

Everyone needs to be involved. Partial commitment to innovation is commitment to failure. There needs to be a willingness to listen to, and act on, the change plan that comes from this consultative innovation process.

Creative Partners' **Andy Radka** shared the results of a survey of 500 top American CEO's. They were asked what their organization needed "to survive in the 21st Century?" Their top answer was ***"to practice creativity and innovation."*** However, ***"only 6% of them believed they were tackling this effectively."***

Quite a gap between expressed needs and application. Obviously blending in a spirit of innovation takes time vs. a quick fix or special seminar.

If innovation and creativity are so important, even critical in business survival; why the gap in application and implementation? While each organization is distinct and different, there needs to be a more holistic, integrated approach to innovation and creativity as a culture.

We need to get *buy-in* on all levels. Further, we need to consider some important points to increase the possibility of idea generation, which in turn drives innovation and creativity in any organization.

What can you do to facilitate this process? Here are some areas of concern in building a foundation for success under this creative and innovative initiative:

Innovation strategy:
Innovation needs to be an *integral part* of all strategies and policies in your organization, not just '*tacked*' on as a quick fix up.

It needs to permeate every department, and every section. Every employee must make it their focus, in part, as they conduct their respective roles.

For example, how much time is spent in the boardroom discussing ongoing innovation strategy? This is where the *rubber hits the road*. Your employees see just how much you are *committed* to this path of action.

Support from top management:
In too many organizations ideas and innovation steps are already at risk at their inception. Poor leadership can look the other way or take the courageous step and stretch out a helping hand to buoy them until they can be worked out and tried in the real world.

Ask yourself, *'Do my managers see themselves as leaders whose role is to '**clear the way' for creativity** or are they simply status quo oriented?'*

Your employees and colleagues are watching for your leadership in this arena. What will your employees *see* when they observe your leadership in action?

Collective mindsets:
Whether we acknowledge it or not, we each have mindsets comprised of beliefs, attitudes, and values that drive or motivate our behaviour. These collective mindsets (e.g. 'can't teach old dogs new tricks or 'my people aren't creative') frequently form barriers to the creative process. They need to be unlocked and unblocked.

Business guru Peter Drucker once said, *"defending yesterday – i.e., not innovating – is far more risky than making tomorrow."*

Make sure your organizational mindset **is not creating** an *immune system* or anti-virus system that automatically rejects or attacks new ideas, processes or challenges to the *status quo* business model. This can be your largest obstacle in embedding creative approaches and applied innovation throughout your organization.

Employees get tools and training:
Are your staff given the tools and the on-going training they need to support a creative climate and innovation?

People and training are crucial to your success, and the training needs to be ongoing and reinforced.

Creativity will not magically flourish with the advent of a few courses or the provision of a *few* creative tools to a *few select* people. Everyone needs to be trained and supported in his or her evolution of understanding and applied learning.

We can help you in this respect. www.ideaman.net

One of my clients has instituted a company-wide internet-based learning system for its 6000 plus employees. Each employee can select the modules that apply to their needs, skill enhancements or department. Their top executives have a yearly learning schedule designed for them!

Knowledge management tools:
Does your organization have an intranet that capitalizes on the strides information technology has brought to the battle for business survival?

I.T. often acts as an enabler, which allows us to break the traditional barriers of function, geography and even hierarchy.

This allows for internet-based sparking of ideas and a chance to engage and bring '*all*' the minds or your various teams into the game. This is how you win! (*For example: A few years back, the Titleist people used 6 of my articles on a new intranet site being set up for their sales staff.*)

What gets measured, gets done – metrics for innovation:
Creativity and innovation can be measured and if so, are done on a more consistent basis. If creativity is rewarded, even more! Intellectual assets can impact heavily on your market value. Consider the differential and costs between hardware and software values?

Creation of an idea pipeline:
Is there an effective innovation process, pipeline, or some form of tracking system for converting ideas into innovative services or new products?

Is everyone on your team committed to feeding this process or pipeline?

Only systematic processes, which incorporate a blend of logical and lateral, thinking tools, can bring creativity and innovation. What are you doing to ensure you *prime the pump* and keep this creative pipeline full and flowing?

Supplier and customer mindsets:
Organizations create a demand for innovative suppliers to be able to serve their clients who are demanding innovative products and services. Ask yourself, "*are your current (and potential) clients able to support a dialogue about inventing your shared future?*"

How about your suppliers and allied professionals? They may not even recognize the future until they see it or are made aware of its possibilities. That in part, is your job in the connection and education process of business.

Just a few thoughts to consider as you follow your quest to increased creativity and applied innovation.

The time to act is now! Innovate or evaporate in the dust of those competitors who saw the need, made the investment and took the lead.

It's your choice! Create Your future!

Ideas At Work! – Priming the creativity pump

Ever notice how some people *seem* to be more creative, innovative or just plain lucky at discovering solutions, or having ideas strike, just when they need them? Ever wonder how they do it, or if they were *born* that way? Wish you could be more creative? You can!

There is a secret, *a process*, which will allow you to access your *diminished* creative spark and start a flow of good ideas from which the great, innovative, break-through ones might be found.

To put it simply, you need to **prime the pump,** by being aware of what is happening.

I went camping one hot August weekend. Lovely place in Northern Alberta nestled beside a clear, cool lake with lots of trees and natural surroundings. Very rustic, and just what I was looking for in my quest to take a *mental break* from two major writing projects I was working on at the moment.

When I say rustic, I mean rustic! **No** showers, quaint out-houses, and a fire pit were all that were provided. Water was available via an old-fashioned manual pump located by the lake that was connected to a well dug 100 feet into the ground.

It took a lot of pumping, lots of noise, action and sweat until a noise was heard *rumbling* deep from the earth.

Water would gush out. Once flowing, it was easy to maintain the flow while you filled your water container. Our minds are like that, deeper than we would expect. Often the best ideas are located way down in our subconscious, waiting to be pumped to the surface.

Using your mental muscles is like priming the pump, as that is what starts the water or ideas flowing. Being *curious* about what is happening around you, reading outside your field, asking questions, *mining* or digging into ideas that interest you – all prime the pump and feed the reservoir from which the break-through, innovative ideas you seek come from.

Creativity seems easy, and it can be; if you are systematic at working your brain. Feed your brain the ideas, the challenges, the opportunities, and lots of facts, background, and other information, and see what *bubbles* to the surface.

But how do you apply this at work? Take a note from some of the other creative people who share in the global market. Perhaps they can teach you something that would be of benefit?

General Electric, under CEO Jack Welsh, for example was famous for *borrowing* ideas from other sources. They were openly researching ideas that could be transferred to their operations and looked at their suppliers, competitors, their various divisions, and other companies in the market for inspiration.

If they saw something that was working, they asked, **"Would this work for us to make us more efficient**

or more competitive?" If the answer was 'yes', they would apply it.

According to their own history, they learned about productivity from Lighting; quick response asset management from Appliances; effectiveness from GE Capital; bullet train cost reduction techniques from Aircraft engines; global accounting management from Accounting.

Wal-Mart taught them direct customer feedback – quick market intelligence. GE learned new product introduction from Toshiba, Chrysler, HP, Toyota, and Yokagaw. Ford and Xerox shared insight on launching quality initiatives.

What have you learned from your competitors, suppliers or even your own personnel or departments lately?

Wal-Mart's success is not product specific. Sam Walton looked to others for ideas and could apply innovation in his various processes for doing business. Walton looked for innovation in supplier relationships, distribution, location and pricing. This allowed him to maintain a competitive advantage in supplying his customers what they wanted, at a price they could afford.

General Motors was the first automobile manufacturer in the world to introduce color to the product mix, which has had some long-lasting benefit for that industry and consumers.

But did you know they also invented consumer credit, which allowed people who'd never owned a car to be able to purchase one. (*Gee, only 1,233 more payments, and it's finally mine,* ☺)

3M, famous for inventing the *post it note*™ (its champion had to fight to get them introduced as there was no demand at the time, or so the *experts* said) has a 30/4 rule in place to encourage its employees to explore new ideas and processes. Simply said, 30% of their sales need to come from products that are less than 4 years old. **Keeps them fresh, and keeps them priming the creativity pumps.** What do you do to keep yourself fresh and primed?

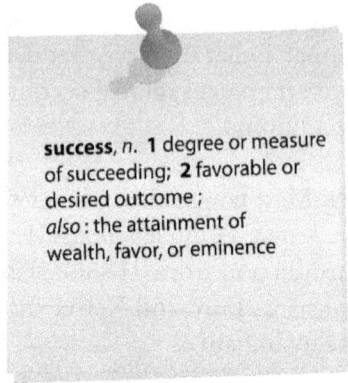

success, *n.* **1** degree or measure of succeeding; **2** favorable or desired outcome ; *also* : the attainment of wealth, favor, or eminence

George **Westinghouse** ran into *conventional wisdom* when he suggested to a few railroad executives that a train could be stopped by using wind. His imagination was unstoppable. Westinghouse Air Brakes soon became conventional equipment on North American trains, and trucks.

George de Mestral noticed the burrs he was brushing out of his wool pants and his dog's coat. He became curious about the tenacity of the burrs. A little observation under a microscope revealed hundreds of tiny hooks snagged in mats of wool and fur. Years later, he made a connection, and the invention of **Velcro ™ fasteners** was born. Einstein would have been proud.

Albert Einstein on creativity, once said, ***"To raise new questions, new possibilities, to regard old problems from a new angle, requires creative imagination. "***

Professor Einstein taught**, three challenges** emerge to priming your creativity pump:
* Think things out fresh… be unconventional
* Destroy the old, and then create the new.
* Tap your imagination. Consider new ideas, ask new questions, raise new possibilities.

Ole *was in love and engaged to be married. One summer he rowed his fiancée across the lake to a little island for a romantic afternoon picnic. They had forgotten the dessert. Ole rowed back, and returned with the dessert. About midpoint, tired, beat, and sweating under the sun and humidity, he stopped to catch his breath. Although the ice cream was melting, his creative processes were engaged. He said, 'There must be an easier way to do this?"*

This prompted the invention of the first portable outboard motor in 1906, with a commercially successful version in 1909. Ole Evinrude got his patent in 1910, and went on to dominate the market for decades. (Gee, wonder if they ever got married?)

Creativity can strike when you least expect it. **Keep priming the creativity pump** and keep your eyes open. You might just surprise yourself and be revealed as a creative leader and thinker!

Picture this… the art of seeing photographically

While taking my architectural training in the 1970's, I pursued the use of a camera to cover some of my education expenses. In addition to being the photo director at NAIT, I took outside assignments for weddings, special functions, meetings and other gatherings, where *'capturing the moment'* was desired by my clients at the time.

I have been able to *'develop'* some of those skills learned as a photographer in my role as an **'idea man'** or creative catalyst for my clients and audiences. These skills have helped me to *'see'* with increased clarity in some of the other areas of my life, my business, and my interaction with those I serve.

There are some interesting parallels between the skill of looking creatively thru the lens of a camera, and the art or skill of creative problem solving or strategic leadership planning.

Photographic creative elements

There are several creative elements that contribute to good photography and they can serve as metaphors for the world of creativity and innovation. Lens selection is just one of them we can draw from for examples.

Most 35mm camera bodies (even the newer digital ones) have interchangeable lenses, which allow us to '*frame*' our subject in a variety of interesting and creative ways:

- **Normal** focal length lens *(comes with the camera as a standard)* allows you to shoot pictures from a perspective very like what you see with your naked eye.

- **Telephoto** lenses *(come in various combinations)* allow you to bring in distant objects by appearing to make them closer. They tend to focus in on one part of the scene and provide a decreased field of view than the normal lens.

- **Wide-angle** lenses take in more of the scene that a normal lens. They tend to emphasize the distances between objects and sometimes distort a bit on the edges.

- **Panoramic** lenses take in a full spectrum shot giving you the 'big picture' view. They tend to take more time, are more susceptible to movement distortion and use more film.

Lighting selection *(natural, augmented)*, shutter or aperture speed can be used to create with a camera too. It is like painting with pictures. Using different lenses allows the photographer to play with elements such as image exposure, lighting, and the shooting angle from which the shot is framed. This allows for some very creative photographs. **Photography is a numbers game.** To come up with a great image, it is preferable to take a many shots with various shutter speeds, and lighting choices. You never know which combination (lens, exposure, point of view, or lighting) will yield the best results. So, you take a large quantity of shots and work toward gleaning some quality results in the selection to follow. Works with smart phones too. Ideas follow that same guideline.

Applying this metaphor to our quest for creative innovation

Creativity, like photography, is all about the skill of '*seeing.*' Being able to approach a situation and look at it differently than everyone else.

During the years, I was designing kitchens, I'd frequently come up with several creative approaches to remodeling a frustrating kitchen or bath area. An area the client had lived with and was finally asking for help in fixing.

Quite often I heard my clients say, **'Why didn't I THINK of That?'** *Perhaps because I was looking at it with a different set of eyes and seeing the possibilities, not the liabilities.* **I was looking for what could be, not what was!** *I hear that at times when I am coaching executives or consulting with companies and organizations. Often, I ask questions that evoke new tracks for thought, simply because I see their situation or business from a different perspective or with 'fresh' eyes. I see what could be, and they are still seeing what is...*

When we analyze a problem or opportunity, we tend to '*focus*' in on a single aspect of it; such as you would with a telephoto lens. At other times our approach may lead us to broaden our intuitive perspective and take in the bigger picture like a wide-angle lens.

And at other times, we need to see how it integrates or fits in with other factors or elements, like a panoramic view would give us.

Often as a photographer, you would walk around your subject seeking the best shot, the best light in which to view it or them. This procedure from a creative process in innovation can yield some fresh ideas and reflective insights. Both the innovator and the photographer recognize the importance of quantity as an approach to quality. **The best way to have a great idea is to have many ideas to choose from.**

A few thoughts to conclude…

If you or your team are looking for methods or techniques to increase your creative output, why not take a tip from the photographic picture book. Resist the trap of looking at your current opportunities or challenges from your normal, habitual, policy-driven viewpoint.

Take a *'mental walk'* around your challenge or opportunity in the context of other forces, trends or insights. Are there similar situations you've faced, or other people in your network have successfully faced in the past? Like the photographer, examine all the variables and factors that just might lead you to a winning solution.

Remember, creativity, like photography, is all about seeing or viewing things differently – about thinking and understanding fluently. Look to see the unique elements and influencing factors that others might have missed from their narrow or normal viewpoint.

Mistakes... leverage for success!

"Crisis can often have value because it generates transformation... I have found that I always learn more from my mistakes than from my successes. If you aren't making some mistakes, you aren't taking enough chances." John Sculley

Like many of you, I hate making mistakes, and worse yet having to admit them and clean up after them. This has often been an area of challenge for me in my growth as a person and in establishing my business. But, I am learning and that is the important thing.

Someone once told me, '*Learn from the mistakes of others, you'll never live long enough to make enough of your own.*'

At the time, that sounded ludicrous to me, as I didn't want to admit my own, let alone discuss them with someone else, or hear about theirs.

A couple of years back I read an article while flying to a speaking engagement in the USA about a company who had tackled this *'mistake-itis'* full-on, and had turned it into a value-added training tool for their company. What they did was invite their management and staff to submit their mistakes and each month they voted on the biggest mistake, and gave a decent cash prize for the *'winner.'*

Here again, initially I thought, *'What a dumb idea!'*

But, as I finished reading the article, I saw the wisdom in their process. What they had discovered was needless repetition of mistakes throughout the company, were costing them needless manpower and additional resources. Someone would make a mistake, fix it, and simply continue without talking about it. In fact, the corporate climate was such that mistakes were not openly discussed. Then someone else would repeat the mistake, and the negative investment cycle would continue.

'A mistake only proves that someone stopped talking long enough to do something.' Michael LeBoeuf

The positive results of developing a culture where mistakes were accepted as a normal part of doing the work and in making progress were amazing. But, the **sharing of the mistakes, and the lessons learned was the key point.**

Sharing the mistakes and the lessons, *leveraged* the learning curve of their management and their staff.

- It allowed them to avoid needless repetition of mistakes, and all the lost time and costly resources that entailed.

43

- It allowed the company to grow and expand on a stronger foundation.

- It encouraged its management and staff to be more open to innovation, and to take *'educated'* risks in developing new business, services and products to serve their changing clientele.

Let me challenge you to do some honest reflection and answer the following questions.

- What was your most recent mistake?

- What did you learn from it?

- Have you shared the *'lesson'* you learned with your team? If not, why not?

One of my biggest lessons in life (business too) was in learning how to not 'recycle' my mistakes. I needed to learn from each one, savour the lesson, and move ahead boldly to make some new mistakes. I also needed to make some new progress from that process!

So, you have a problem...that's great!

So, you have a problem, that's great! Are you crazy? Actually...NO! Someone once told me that, *"I'd get paid or determine my value, by my ability to solve problems. "*

If it was easy, everyone would be doing it, and the competition would be intense. But, as most customers will tell you, most businesses are '*not*' in the problem-solving field. Your ability to solve your client's problems will be directly related to the number of sales and continued growth of your firm. The more successfully, and **creatively you and your staff solve these problems**, the more referrals and fans you'll see. The more productive you are personally in being a solution-oriented executive, or employee will dramatically affect your paycheck and career path. These ideas will work with your staff challenges as well.

I've learned to apply this **simple 4-stage process for dealing with problems**. I've found this to be an effective way to deal **creatively** with customer complaints and concerns as well as other areas of your business and life. These ideas also work with creative and strategic planning, or in everyday problem solving.

Since so many of my clients and audiences have a need to be productive in dealing with customers, I've written from that perspective. This section is adapted from my book, *'Make ME Feel Special – Idea-rich customer service strategies'* (www.SuccessPublications.ca)

- Invest time in making sure you **UNDERSTAND** the problem.
- The key to understanding is to **IDENTIFY** the real cause.
- Take time to fully explore and **DISCUSS** all the possible solutions.
- Take action to **SOLVE** or fully resolve the problem.

The secret to growing your business to the next level is to go through this process with your employees so they can do so with your clients. After the problem, has been successfully resolved, **go the extra mile**. This means doing something unexpected to assist the client or to show them you appreciate the opportunity to prove your commitment to their well-being. This will help turn an angry or frustrated client into a fan, or better yet...a champion for your business.

Stage One:

Understanding the problem: normally a problem is in a perception of a '*difference*' of what we expected to happen and what happened. Here are **3 action steps** to help.

- **Gather ALL the facts**. Be thorough and investigate. Let the client talk!
- **Listen carefully** and don't be defensive. Wait until they've finished talking and ask more questions to draw them out to find out their REAL concerns.
- **Rephrase** or repeat the problem back to the client to make sure you've heard it correctly and understand what needs to be resolved. Agree on this stage.

It's important at this stage to make sure you don't fall into the trap of denying or trying to avoid the problem. Or worse yet, blaming or attacking someone else or demonstrating the same negative emotions in response to a customer's complaint. **Listen and get the facts!**

Stage Two:
Identify the Cause of the Problem: You might ask yourself or your client a few questions to find out what may have caused the problem.

- **What has happened?** Listen and ask questions. Get a true assessment of the current situation.
- **What should have happened?** Ask questions and listen carefully. Was perception a problem in this situation? What were they expecting?
- **What went wrong?** This is where you start partnering with the client.

Keep in mind the true cost of an unhappy client. What future purchases (*life time value*) could you expect from this client? What future business this client could influence? What the problem at hand costs to rectify? (*Hint: average cost is 8-16 customers lost for each unsatisfied customer.*) Not taking the time to '*fully*' satisfy a customer concern can cost you big time.

From experience, problems generally often fall into **4 major areas:**

- **Mechanics or Function** - product or service failed to work as expected.
- **Assembly or use** - someone didn't use it correctly or put it together incorrectly.

- **The People Factor** - we make mistakes in how we do something or how we deal with a client. Happens frequently in business as it is an inexact science.
- **Client EGO** - how this PROBLEM makes them look (good or bad) in their eyes and the eyes of their friends and families.

Stage Three:
Explore and DISCUSS possible solutions. This is possibly the most critical part in the client satisfaction /problem solving process. Here is where we need to '*fully*' focus and objectively look at the challenge we've partnered with the client to solve. Again, a few **action steps**. As a leader or coach, you can follow this path as well.

- **Suggest options**. Take time to explore ALL the options that might effectively help solve this problem or at least minimize the impact.
- **Ask your customer for their ideas**. Very often, they have a solution in mind, or have some good input that will help you mutually resolve it to their satisfaction. If they are a partner in the decision, they will help make it work and will be more inclined to be happier with the results. **Their satisfaction will result in referrals for you!**
- **Agree on the best solution or course of action**. After you've fully explored the options, make sure you both agree on what and when you will do to resolve it. **THEN DO IT!**

Stage Four:
Take ACTION to resolve the problem. This is the completion stage that builds a foundation for a potential long-term relationship with your formerly dissatisfied client. Make this a priority focus for your firm. Once you've agreed on what needs to be done, move heaven and earth to do it, and do it better and quicker than you've promised. Remember, they are watching to make sure you were serious about making them happy. This is your chance to prove your commitment.

Again, **three action steps.**

- **Physically remove the cause of the problem** or take steps to retrain if personnel.
- **Take corrective action** to substitute, replace or repair the product or service.
- **Ask the client** if they are satisfied with the changes and action you've taken.

Going the extra mile. This is where you cement the relationship by doing something extra, something totally unexpected by the client. Show them you care and are concerned about the inconvenience they've experienced. **Apply your creativity to cementing the relationship!**

Use your complaints as a creative source of product or service development. Each one is an opportunity for you to learn how to better serve your clients, refine your service, or improve your product in the market place.

This is also an opportunity to expand your business or service by using these creative solutions as stepping-stones or business building blocks.

Yesterday's problems are today's new and improved products or services. Want to be a creativity leader? YES! Then learn from each lesson your clients give you. This is an opportunity for you to build a strong foundation for success well into the next millennium.

Don't miss the lesson. It might be a "v-e-r-y" valuable one!

A personal note from Bob

I share with you some creative new approaches to problem solving or strategic planning. I appreciate the opportunity to exercise my creativity and learn together with my audiences. Often, the lessons we discuss, and the ideas generated help me in refining my approach and my program content.

I challenge you to use these tips and techniques in your day-to-day operations, as well as in your personal life. I think you'll find them helpful.

Remember there is always a creative solution!
Share these ideas with your clients and co-workers, so they can take advantage of ways to make their lives more productive and less stressful.

Hint: Leaders and Coaches act as catalysts and conduits for learning.

Mental vitamins and brain exercises

The mind works best when challenged with a daily routine of creative thinking; just like an exercise program is designed to tone and condition the body's muscles.

The late **Earl Nightingale**, noted self-help expert, devised a very **simple method that only requires three things**:

- An open mind
- A pencil or pen
- A pad of paper or something to write on.

Here is the system or method he devised that works as well today, as it did when he introduced it to his readers and listeners a long time ago.

Give your subconscious a pressing problem to digest and gnaw on just before you go to sleep. Spend 20-30 minutes thinking about a challenge, problem, or opportunity you are dealing with currently. When you lay down forget about it. While you sleep your subconscious mind, the source of most breakthrough ideas, will be mulling it over and thinking about it from various perspectives and sides.

Wake up an hour before anyone else. Find a comfortable place to sit, get a coffee or juice, a pad of paper, and a pencil or pen.

Relax and let the ideas flow. Write everything down as the ideas occur, no matter how wild, far out or seemingly impractical they seem. Don't stop to edit or judge these ideas, just capture or record them.

Let your mind do a *'mental dump'* onto paper into a form you can do something with later.

This simple *'solo'* brainstorming method worked like a charm for Earl, on a regular basis; and produced some outstanding ideas, which he later launched successfully. According to Earl, the key is the subconscious mind, which acts like a gigantic warehouse for ideas and thoughts, floating around just below our conscious mind awareness. Insights or hunches are ideas, which simply bubbled up from the vast reservoir of our subconscious mind.

While you are studying, or feeding your mind, a problem or outlining an opportunity just before you go to sleep is like stuffing your subconscious mind. This feeds your powerful brain new fresh material to play with and from which to work.

Try this simple form of personal brainstorming… you might inspire yourself with the wisdom you draw from your subconscious mind.

Creative problem-solving

Many teams find that a more creative, less rigid approach to solving problems often yields the highest quality solution. However, first each needs to understand what factors make creative thinking work best. Otherwise known as the '***association of ideas***,' creative thinking is the process by which imagination feeds off memory and knowledge to cause one idea to lead to another.

This section will help individuals identify what factors are necessary for a productive creative problem-solving session, and to provide a process for thinking creatively. It will also give your group an opportunity to practice some creative thinking skills.

Requirements for Creative Thinking

The key factors that influence team success in any creative thinking session are:

Suspend Judgment
By far the most important characteristic of effective creative problem solving is to have an open mind. Your team should work on creating a supportive environment where judgment and criticism are not permissible. Like the process of brainstorming, these qualities stifle creativity.

Self-Assessment
To develop a more open mind, it may help to determine your tendency to cling dogmatically to your ideas and opinions.

Develop a Positive Attitude

Have enthusiasm and optimism for ideas, even if they seem wild and unrealistic. Develop an attitude that all ideas are good ideas, as cynicism will only inhibit creative thinking.

Use Checklists

There are a couple reasons why your team should write down EVERY idea, no matter how far-fetched. First, it sends the message to the team that everyone's ideas are valued and helps create a supportive environment. Second, recording all ideas will ensure that nothing important is forgotten and give the team an opportunity to go back and combine parts of one idea with parts of another, letting ideas feed off each other.

Be Self Confident

Remember that many of the world's greatest ideas were ridiculed at first. **Have faith in your creativity!!!** Some of our most basic scientific principles like that the Earth is round and revolves around the sun, never would have been advanced without the confidence and courage to go against the grain.

Encourage Others

Praise and encouragement are the fuel for creativity; it enables ideas to flow freely and motivates team members. Instead of criticizing or rejecting an idea, offer praise and encourage your team to keep up the good work!

The creative thinking process

Here is a summary of the stages of creative thinking. These stages resemble the steps in the reflective approach to problem solving, with adjustments to encourage creativity and exploit brainstorming.

Stages in Creative Problem Solving

Orientation

This step of the creative thinking process is a matter of setting the stage for a productive session, i.e., making sure you have all the necessary requirements for an open and creative group process-if necessary, review the information in the previous topic. In addition, the team should generate a list of topics or headings for which it plans to gather ideas.

Preparation and Analysis

This stage is primarily devoted to **fact-finding**. While gathering, facts is important, it is only necessary to gather those facts that will serve to further creative thinking. Getting bogged down in too many details at this stage may restrain creative thinking efforts. There will be time later to go back and fill in the facts you need as you go.

Go back to the headings you generating in the orientation phase. Are there any headings that don't seem relevant to your task now? Focus on gathering facts for those topics that will help you identify causes for the problem you are trying to solve. You might also research successful past solutions to similar problems.

Analyzing the data, you have collected is an important part of helping to reveal clues to the solution. It is primarily geared toward establishing relationships among the facts you have collected. Look for similarities, differences, and causes by asking questions like **"*What does this fact have in common with that fact?*"** or **"*How are these things different?*"** and **"*What would cause this effect?*"** Analyzing data in this way will help you develop a framework for generating solution.

One final note about fact-finding is to be sensitive to the distinction between those topics that will require an immediate decision, and those that will require *'creative'* thinking and financing. For example, if cost is a concern to your team, find out exactly how much money is available for your task.

This is a decision that must be made considering available resources, whereas developing a solution that fits within your budgetary constraints will require creative thinking.

Brainstorming

The philosophy behind brainstorming is that the more ideas there are on the table, the more likely a suitable solution will emerge. This stage of the process is a "freewheeling" exchange of ideas to get together a list of as many possibilities as you can.

Remember to write all ideas down, no matter how far-fetched they may seem, and to maintain an open mind at all times. Let ideas feed off one another and feel free to combine parts of one solution with another or alter ideas in various ways.

Incubation
Incubation is the "time-out" stage of the process in which group members disperse for a period to let ideas grow and to encourage "illumination" of the correct solution. While a time-out may not always be practical for every problem-solving team, it is nonetheless considered an important part of the creative process so as not to let creativity lag by overworking the mind.

Whether the time-out is a lunch-break, a good night's sleep, or a week hiatus before the next meeting, the purpose should be not to force the mind to think about any aspect of the problem or solution, but to let the mind meander as it wants. Some of the world's most creative people rely on these moments of silence and solitude for their best ideas, and if it is at all possible for the team to take a break from its task, incubation should be incorporated into its activities.

Synthesis and Verification
Out of all the possibilities the team has generated during its brainstorming session, the ideal solution should be a combination of the best qualities of each idea. While during the orientation and analysis phases of the process the teams', job was to break apart the problem, the task at hand now is to construct a whole out of the ideas generated by brainstorming.
One good way to do this is to make a list of all the desirable qualities or disadvantages that a solution might have, and then rate each idea generated.

Each quality or disadvantage can be weighted in terms of its importance or applied without weighting. The idea with the best overall profile can then be identified. A second way of synthesizing ideas is to create an outline or grouping of ideas, with similar ideas assigned to the same group and relations between groups of ideas mapped out.

Verification is the final phase of the process and requires testing the solution the team has chosen to see if it achieves all the team's goals. I hope you find some of these ideas of value.

Business observations on applied creativity

When teaching this program in person I often pull examples from business to illustrate creative techniques. Many of these you know, but they still ring true.

Telus, AT&T, and the satellite or cable outlets taught how to take a basic service and bundle items clients want for a higher rate. What can you bundle?
Starbucks took an espresso machine previously seen in Italian and European coffee shops and built and empire around the world selling their 'experience'.
Canadian trapper, **Charles Birdseye** observed that the fish he caught during the winter froze quickly. When he cooked them they still tasted fresh. This observant concept was the start of the frozen food industry.
Federal Express applied an idea (central hub) used by banks in clearing checks and documents as the basis for an effective and efficient delivery system.

Reflective problem-solving

No decision-making team follows the same procedure for solving problems as another team. Regardless of how you and your team members approach a problem, however, most high-quality decisions are reached by performing certain functions.

Reflective problem-solving emphasizes the importance of **basic tasks: defining concepts, identifying needs, and identifying and evaluating solutions.** Groups using reflective problem solving make sure to cover an agenda of these key tasks, usually in a standard order. This section will give you a brief checklist of tasks and suggestions about how to organize discussion effectively to address them.

Problem-solving tasks

There are **five key points involved in problem solving**:

1. **Define the problem**: Make a list of resources -- people, books, web sites, etc. -- that have some connection to, and information about the problem you are trying to solve. Use these resources to clarify any unfamiliar terms or concepts and to clarify for the group what you understand the problem to be. At this point you are **looking for symptoms, evidence that a problem exists, not causes,** which in the next step will explain why a problem exists.

2. **Analyze the problem**: After the group, has discussed the evidence for the existence of the problem and defined what that problem is, you can now turn your attention to analyzing the evidence more thoroughly, **looking for relevant data** that may explain why the problem exists. This step in the procedure is a matter of evaluating the data you've collected and the sources it comes from. Problem Solving Activity 1 will help you master good rules for evaluating sources.

3. **Establish criteria for evaluating solutions**: Set an objective with your group that all proposed solutions should strive for. Based on your definition of the problem and analysis of its cause(s), this objective should be the **one specific goal that any acceptable solution should attain**. If the problem you are trying to solve is too complex to set only one objective, another means for establishing criteria to evaluate solutions is to make a list of MUSTS/WANTS.

MUSTS are those basic requirements without which the solution would be unacceptable.

WANTS are those qualities that are desirable in any solution and should be prioritized from most desirable to least desirable. This type of checklist may help your group maximize the effectiveness of any solution without omitting any essential requirements.

4. **Propose solutions**: After you have established some basis for evaluating solutions, try brainstorming solutions. From the list of solutions that emerge from your brainstorming session, develop a realistic range of

solutions and select the one that best fits your needs according to your evaluation criteria.

5. **Take action**: Write an action plan that details the steps that need to be taken to implement your solution and the resources needed to do it.

The way your group performs these necessary problem-solving tasks is incidental, so long as you address each function. Some groups find it helpful to follow a more detailed and systematic process for problem-solving to help keep them focused.

If you and your team members are having difficulty staying on track, following this step-by-step process -- keeping in mind the essential tasks outlined above -- may help you reach your goal more efficiently and effectively.

Organizing discussion

Problem solving groups tend to encounter a set of common trouble areas. The following attitudes and strategies will help your team can avoid these trouble areas,

Avoid focusing too much attention on solutions prematurely. Refrain from acting on the first suggestion of a solution before the problem has been thoroughly defined, its causes discussed, and a range of solutions evaluated. Don't fall for the '*first right*' answer.

Don't avoid problems. Many people dodge problem-solving activities because they have a low tolerance for uncertainty. This can lead to a *"quick-fix"* attitude that seeks to eliminate the problem as quickly as possible by whatever means necessary.

Work on cultivating endurance for ambiguity and doubt and become actively involved in the entire problem-solving process.

Refrain from dogmatism and fixating on ideas. At all times maintain an open mind and be willing to consider new problems and new ideas.

Be careful of your own biases and the biases of other sources when evaluating the facts of a case. The challenge is objective investigation and judgement.

Don't make sweeping generalizations of accepted facts or beliefs without sufficient evidence that comes from reliable sources.

Don't misinterpret honest disagreement for dislike. Recognize that group members all have different backgrounds, values, experiences, and thinking styles that have significant bearing on how an individual views a problem.

When someone expresses a different opinion, or disagrees with you, don't take it as a *'personal attack.'* **View this difference in opinion as a *'positive'* consequence of the group's diversity that will help everyone *'think'* through the problem more carefully.** It really is an indication of a creative, healthy team!

Thunder-thinking… when lightning strikes

"The lightning spark of thought generation in the solitary mind awakens its likeness in another mind," Thomas Carlyle

Is there a way to increase my productivity and leverage my creativity? Is it true that two minds are better than one? Are there advantages to working with others to brainstorm my ideas, problems, and dreams? Yes, and it is an easily acquired skill!

Thunder-thinking occurs when you unleash your mind's creative power, and is fully experienced when the lightning (***illumination)*** of a new idea strikes. But can this creative power be controlled or directed? Again, yes it can!

In both my personal and business experience, I've found that unleashing the creative power of 'several' minds on a single issue can work miracles.

There are many benefits to teaming up for creative problem solving. It can be a lot of fun and bring people closer together, providing a sense of belonging or bonding that enhances relationships and creativity. Morale can be enhanced when people are solicited for their input and ideas. A larger amount of good ideas, better ideas, will result if the *'thunder-thinking'* process is properly utilized. Communication is often dramatically improved.

Webster's defines 'brainstorming' as a group problem-solving technique that involves the 'spontaneous contribution of ideas from all members of the group'.

I've been told that Hindu teachers in India practiced it over 400 years ago. It works as a part of the creative

problem-solving process, occurring during the idea generation or illumination phase. **'Thunder-thinking'** more accurately focuses this power for productive tapping into your creative genius.

The creative problem-solving guide is a tri-phase process involving **fact finding**, i.e. gathering information, doing research and defining the problem. This is followed by the **idea generation** phase, as mentioned already. The final phase is the **solution selection**, i.e. refining, verification of ideas and selection of the best possible alternative idea or combination of ideas.

Keep in mind that ideas generated during a 'thunder-thinking' session need to be evaluated and processed to be productive in their application. **Thunder-thinking** as a creative process provides its greatest benefit in the generation of good ideas, in contrast to our experience in a typical meeting, and in less time too!

The typical committee is not '*normally*' a breeding ground for creativity, with participants continually getting bogged down in minutia or in defending their own agenda or viewpoints. I remember a quote that sums it up, *"God so loved the world that he didn't send a committee."* This is not to down play the valid contribution of committees, but to emphasize their limitations and difference in roles unless they are focused on creative exercises and challenging people to think. Over the years, I've served on some very productive committees.

Are there any rules I should be aware of, you ask?
Yes! These will assist in effective thunder-thinking.

1. **Criticism and judgment are suspended**...virtually forbidden. Only by suspending judgement do we unleash the power of our individual minds and tap into the real underlying power of SYNERGY. Evaluate later.
2. **Freethinking or wheeling is essential.** No idea is too wild, too crazy, or too far-fetched when it comes to attacking the matter at hand. Evaluate later.
3. **Shoot for quantity!** Make it your goal to throw out as many ideas as possible. The greater number generated the greater chance of discovering a useful idea.
4. **Work to combine and build on ideas, to improve on them, to add to them**, as they are mentioned. Encourage participants to value add or layer on the ideas of others as they add new ones of their own.

Work each idea and adaptation until it reaches a natural pause and then move on to the next one.

In addition, these following **guidelines** will help.

1. **Make the problem to be brainstormed as specific as possible**, by breaking it down into its essential components. Focus each participant's energies on a single topic. Accurate problem definition will assist in its solution being generated.
2. **Use thunder-thinking for idea finding decisions**. Judgement style decisions work better with a balance sheet or pro vs con approach.
3. Once you've defined the problem to be brainstormed, **share the relevant background and parameters with all participants.**
4. Start each session with a **review and a commitment by all parties to follow the basic rules and guidelines.**
5. **Work to side step a "perfectionistic" atmosphere** ... keep it informal and fun. A spirit of friendly competition could be helpful. Encourage ideas that are stimulated by previous ideas...get a chain reaction happening...feed or bounce off each other's creativity and ingenuity.

I find it helpful to appoint one 'non-participant' to act as a recorder, to ensure ideas are captured for future evaluation. Take turns if you want. This will also ensure participants are not bogged down in the recording process. Focus your energies instead on the creative process.

Avoid these following thunder-thinking blockers, i.e. common phrases that kill the creative process and limit open discussion and idea generation. Be wary if you start hearing them from people on your team, family or work associates!
1. That is ridiculous.
2. We don't have the time
3. That's not included in our responsibility.
4. Let's form a committee. (My favorite!)
5. What will the union (or Management, or…) say?
6. Why change it when it's still working?
7. It's not in the budget…
8. Has anyone else tried it before?
9. We've never done that before.
10. We're not ready for that.

Add your own. Make sure you don't fall into these traps. Too often, we slip into negative thinking, even during a positive - creative period. This can seriously undermine the process!

Why does it work? Its essential success is with the chain reaction process. Idea stimulation in the host brain as well as the participant's brains. The associative power of ideas generates a two-way current. When you offer up a new idea, your own imagination - along with everyone else's - is stimulated (*like sharing stories or jokes brings yours to mind.*) People tend to generate more ideas with other people, in social settings, than they do individually.

Associative idea generation tests have indicated a production increase of over 65% in social sessions, over solo efforts.

Creative competition can work wonders, with mental output increases by up to 50%.

The major difference in the concept of **thunder-thinking** is in its acceptance of ALL ideas. This rules out the possibility of any premature criticism or judgement stifling the creative problem- solving process. Thunder-thinking remains effective when all participants follow the basic rules and guidelines.

Can I hold thunder-thinking or creative problem-solving sessions with only two people?

Yes, although the more the merrier. Ideally 3-10 people can become an idea generation machine. It can, however, be done with as few as two people. A good partner can stimulate effort in addition to increased associative powers.

There are a few **guidelines to keep in mind, which apply to two person creative teams** as well as larger thunder thinking groups.

1.   **Ensure there is an incentive for each party.** Work to see that values and paybacks are equitable or compatible for each of you.
2.   **Select a specific place and scheduled time to think.** Allow time for each of you to rethink the problem. Allow the information to incubate in your subconscious brain prior to each meeting.
3.   **Get together,** as planned, to thunder-think the problem. Try to keep it fun and informal... bounce ideas off each other. Keep the atmosphere informal and accepting to ensure the idea flow continues.

Consider each idea generated. Go for quantity and record them for future evaluation and decision. I've used a tape recorder to make sure I didn't miss any good ones.

4. **Take a break** ... think alone. Review all your joint ideas to date. Do additional research and formulate your ideas.

5. **Get back together, review ideas and generate new ones**. Start choosing alternatives found satisfactory to both parties.

This is where your judgement, preferences and personal tastes come into play. This will often result in at least '*one*' workable idea.

Remember not to argue! This is the deathblow to the power of creative problem solving. Too many potentially good ideas die on the drawing boards or in the embryonic phase if argumentative atmospheres emerge. It's not about right and wrong ... it is about better solutions.

Intelligent discussion is great! Argument is a dream killer and should be avoided at all costs. As phrased by Robert Quillen, *"Discussion is an exchange of knowledge, argument is an exchange of ignorance."*

We want to work with each other to achieve feats not grasped alone. This goal should allow us to supersede our individual egos, to reach better results in our lives.

Break Out-of-the-Box Thinking

This will jog your problem-solving skills. You can create novel ideas by **NOT** following expectations, rules, regulations, assumptions, or long-standing traditions, company history or policy. Go against the grain and the status quo to find the ultimate solution you need.

Just for a moment, **remove the '*speed limits*' from your mind** and challenge your traditional linear thinking. Ask yourself a few *strategic* questions to trigger your creative juices.

Look at your problem or idea and ask yourself some questions.

This will allow you to change the way you look at them. **A slight change in *perspective* can productively change your results.**

Take a moment and ask yourself:

- What if?
- If only?
- Why not?
- Who says?
- Does it apply to me?
- By whose standards?
- Is there another way?

Continue asking yourself:

Let's pretend for a minute we had *all* the resources, personnel, and time?

- Is there a second '*right*' answer?
- What happens if I do nothing?
- What is the best that can happen?
- What is the worst that can happen?
- How can I benefit or learn from this experience?

Just a few mind joggers to help kick start your thinking process.

Take a few minutes and write some answers that relate to your goal or problem at hand. Your answers should be based or relate to the earlier statements.

Take advantage of opportunities

Business success at its basic essence is based on innovation, solving problems, or fulfilling the needs, wants, and desires of our clients.

Here's a potpourri sampler of how to take advantage of opportunities to expand or unlock your business potential.

- What business are you REALLY in? Keep asking this question and keep adapting your business to keep it fresh. Hint: think in terms of customer benefits. What do your customers get when they deal with you? What do they really want?

- Combine two or more products or services to create a new one. Perhaps you can work with a strategic partner or ally to develop a new service or product that will bring mutual benefit?

- Take an idea from another industry and transfer it, or adapt to suit yours and the needs of your clients. (For example: air miles/coffee cards/buy 10 get one free promotions.)

- Try something that didn't work the FIRST time. It might now; with changes in technology, resources, client needs and attitudes.

- Take advantage of the trends or changing interest in the market place. This is where your customer service focus will help, a lot!

- Use a different material or process to do a traditional job. Creativity counts!

- Look for ways to be a value-added company or person, focusing on real customer service. How can you personally make changes to what you bring to your work?

Being creative is often as simple as being, and being willing to risk by trying new or unfamiliar things and activities. Creativity is what solves your problems and builds your long-term business. Looking at your business with fresh eyes, and from different perspectives is one secret in tapping your inner genius and accessing your Creative S.O.U.L.

Thinking in reverse

When setting your goals, **Steven Covey** suggests that we should **"begin with the end in mind."** Wouldn't solving this problem be a worthy goal? Focus on the end-result or desired result.

Take your time and define it carefully. Ask questions that eventually lead you carefully, step by step, back to the current state of affairs or situation. In business, it can be called reverse engineering, but it works every time.

Define your ideal solution or desired outcome. Be as accurate and descriptive as you can.

Keep asking yourself, *"If this is the case, what would have to happen to get this result?"* and use that as your next reverse step. Usually you will find the path within 10 to 12 steps. Try it, you might just enjoy it!

1. _____ Ideal solution or desired outcome

    2. _____ next step (backward)

        3. _____next step (backward)

            4. _____next step (backward)

                5. _____next step

                    6. ____next step

                      7. __present

Success keys from Rubbermaid

Rubbermaid is a pretty successful company, generating more than 2.3 billion in retail sales. Not bad for a company who creates consumable products and take-for-granted ones for a multitude of uses.

Rubbermaid in their own words, seeks to **"*Master the mundane.*"** They create storage products for the house, the garage, and the patio, anywhere something that needs to be durable, water-proof, and cost effective. Their aim in creating all these '*mundane*' products is to promote, **'Consumer delight!'** They apply the **5 T's** in their creative design and discussion process:

- **Trends:** Be aware of what is happening in the world.
- **Teams:** Harness the power of applied teamwork toward a focused goal.
- **Training:** Offer training to equip your teams to succeed.
- **Technology:** Acquire and learn technology to make what you do easier and to expand your ability to be creative and innovative.
- **Creative Tension:** Tension can be a good thing if applied creatively. Feed the process!

They even have **Trend Messengers** whose role it is to gather information from around the world around them and share their observations with the rest of their team.

They've developed **seven success keys or operating principles**, which have helped them reach their present success and will, no doubt, continue to do so:

1. **Cross-functional teams** are more reliably productive.
2. **Oversight teams**, drawn from the Company's top executives, supervise every business unit.
3. **Company-wide business councils** focus on performance and innovation in such business practices as marketing and design.
4. **Scrutinize market trends** by keeping close watch on surface action and digging well beneath the surface for what customers are buying, or would buy.
5. **Don't waste time on run-of-the-mill research**. Look for a need, impact and invest $.
6. **Impose creative tension**; inspire their people to come up with 'fresh' solutions to new tasks in new environments.
7. **Offer every kind of training**, but leave it to individual associates to take advantage of it.

Can you learn from this successful creator of home, garage and industrial products? Can you, like Rubbermaid, investigate the world around you and see opportunities to expand what you offer your clients, and grow to the next level? My guess would be yes!

Are you applying, or can you apply some of these operating principles in your organization? What would be the response from your team if you did? Would they be more creative and able to explore opportunities for growth and innovation? What do you have to lose? **When will you start this process?**

How to handle the Idea Killers in your life!

YOU have this great dream, or this fantastic idea bursts into your head. You're excited about the unlimited possibilities and can't wait to share it with your co-workers, closest friends and family.

What is their reaction? All too often, their initial reaction is to ridicule the idea; to point out its flaws; to remind us about our lack of education, our lack of money, our lack of experience; or to point out how so and so tried it and it didn't work. The result, too often, you let your dreams die, be minimized, or give up on them. You let your colleagues, friends and family rob you of your future, and your potential for greatness!

Why do they do that? Well it might be for a variety of reasons, some of them with the best intentions. It might simply be their concern to see you avoid getting hurt, or to side-step what they see as a path to failure. It may be, and often is, based on their own fears projected to your action and life. It might be due to a personal failure on their part and a fear that, if you succeed, they will lose you. Or a fear they must deal with the reality that, just maybe, they could have done something about their "*seemingly impossible*" situation. Your potential for success scares them or makes them a bit nervous about their own chances or inactivity.

How do we handle these '*helpers*' or **'*idea killers*'** in our life? One of the best ways I know is to be aware of their existence and seek to avoid them in areas of vulnerability.

I don't mean to cut them off completely. Just realize that they are not committed to, or understanding of, your dreams and desires. Make a conscious choice to keep these areas private, especially during the embryonic or incubation stages of establishing your goals, dreams, or ideas. Maintain your focus, and keep moving forward to seeing your idea or dream become a reality. As someone wrote, **"Show no regrets for the past, no fear for the future. Expect to win! It's a funny thing in life, if you refuse to accept anything but the best, you often get it."**

We may not choose our family, but we do have full control over our friends and over the amount of time we spend with colleagues, friends, and family. This is where we make the decisions that help shape or determine our destiny. In life, there are those who would kill our dreams and those who would, if asked, help nurture our dreams. We can identify and choose each group in which to associate and productively invest our time.

One of the most effective ways of dealing with an idea killer is by **doing your homework**. If you have researched your dream and have done your due diligence, some can even be brought around to being at least a neutral observer.

In the mid 80's I belonged to The Entrepreneurs Association. **Our Credo was:**
"I do not choose to be a common man (or woman). It is my right to be uncommon, if I can. I seek opportunity, not security! I do not wish to be a kept citizen, humbled and dulled by having the

state took after me. I want to take the calculated risk, to dream and to build, to fail and to succeed. I refuse to barter incentive for a dole. I prefer the challenges of life to the guaranteed existence; the thrill of fulfillment to the stale calm of utopia.

I will not trade freedom for beneficence, nor my dignity for a handout. I will NEVER cower before any master, nor bend to any threat. It is my heritage to stand erect, proud and unafraid; to think and act for myself, to enjoy the benefit of my creations and to face the world boldly and say, 'This with God's help, I have done. 'All this is what it means to be an Entrepreneur."

Entrepreneur Magazine was initially our Association publication

Use feedback from these Idea killers as mirrors to show you your blind spots. Often, they see things that you might miss in the heat of passion. Keep in mind their input is for **information only** and check it for accuracy before you allow it to impact your decisions.

Demonstrate by your actions, that you're committed to seeing this project through to completion. Often our past track record of starting and not completing projects may influence their support and enthusiasm. This is especially true with immediate family members.

Idea killers may occasionally become allies, but it takes massive work on your part to win them over to your team. **Keep focused on your Goals and Dreams!**

Don't let another person's critical attitude determine your worth or your future. You don't know how high you can fly until you spread your wings and take to the sky. Please don't let another person's limiting beliefs, no matter how well-intentioned, stop you attempting to dream big, to compete for the ultimate prize ... achieving your personal or professional dream.

It is too easy for those around you, who are hopelessly mired in their own mediocrity, to criticize you for trying to follow your dream, or acting to implement your great idea.

Theodore Roosevelt, who was often criticized, wrote, *"It is not the critic who counts, not the man who points out how the strong man stumbled, or where the doer of deeds could have done them better. The CREDIT belongs to the man (or woman) who is actually in the arena, who strives valiantly - who knows the great enthusiasm, the great devotion ... and spends himself (or herself) in a worthy cause. Who at best, knows the triumph of high achievement; and at the worst, if he (or she) fails ... at least fails while daring greatly, so that his (or her) place shall never be with those cold and timid souls ... who know neither victory nor defeat."*

If you are to get criticism, and you will, let it be for following your own leadership and daring to set your goals higher and build your dreams. Take a lesson and a sage tip from me and, **Remember, they don't build monuments to critics. Create your own future!**

Thanks for reading 'Create Your Future'

Each time I prepare to step on the stage; each time I sit down to write or in this case to re-write, I am challenged to deliver something that will be of use-it-now value to my audiences.

I ask myself, *"If I was reading this, what value would I be looking for?"*
As well as, *"Why is this relevant to me, today?"*

Thanks for investing in yourself and this mini success workbook. These two questions help to keep me focused and clear on my objectives. They help to remind me to dig into my experiences, stories, examples, and research to provide solid information that will be of benefit and help our readers, when they apply it, succeed. That can be an exciting challenge!

I trust we have done that for you in this updated primer to enhance your skills. **'Create Your Future'** is my attempt to capture some of the lessons learned first-hand from observing and working with some tremendously effective leaders and to share them with you. I'd love to hear from you and read your success stories. If you would be so kind, please drop me a quick email at: bob@ideaman.net

Bob 'Idea Man' Hooey
2011 Spirit of CAPS recipient
www.ideaman.net;
www.HaveMouthWillTravel.com

(Bob pictured at the Phillips factory in Holland)

Connect with me on:

Facebook: www.facebook.com/bob.hooey
LinkedIn:
www.linkedin.com/in/canadianideamanbobhooey
YouTube: www.youtube.com/ideamanbob
Smashwords:
www.smashwords.com/PROfile/view/Hooey
Follow me on **Twitter:** @IdeamanHooey
Snail mail: Box 10, Egremont, Alberta T0A0Z0

About the author

Bob 'Idea Man' Hooey is a charismatic, confident leader, corporate trainer, inspiring facilitator, Emcee, prolific author, and award winning motivational keynote speaker on leadership, creativity, success, business innovation, and enhancing team performance.

Using personal stories drawn from rich experience, he challenges his audiences to engage his **Ideas At Work!** – To act on what they hear, with clear, innovative building-blocks and field-proven success techniques to increase their effectiveness.

Bob challenges them to hone specific 'success skills' critical to their personal and professional advancement. Bob outlines real-life, results-based, innovative ideas personally drawn from 29 plus years of rich leadership experience in retail, construction, small business, entrepreneurship, manufacturing, association, consulting, community service, and commercial management.

Bob's conversational, often humorous, professional, and sometimes-provocative style continues to inspire and challenge his audiences across North America. Bob's motivational, innovative, challenging, and practical Ideas At Work! have been successfully applied by thousands of leaders and professionals across the globe.

Bob is a frequent contributor to North American consumer, corporate, association, trade, and on-line publications on leadership, success, employee motivation and training; as well as creativity and innovative problem solving, priority and time management, and effective customer service. He is the inspirational author of 30 plus publications, including several best-selling, print, e-books, reader style e-pubs, and a Pocket Wisdom series. Visit: **www.SuccessPublications.ca** for more information.

Retired, award winning kitchen designer, Bob Hooey, CKD-Emeritus was one of only 75 Canadian designers to earn this prestigious certification by the National Kitchen and Bath Association.

In December 2000, Bob was given a special CAPS National Presidential award "…for his energetic contribution to the advancement of CAPS and **his living example of the power of one**" in addition to being elected to the CAPS National Board.

He has been recognized by the National Speakers Association and other professional groups for his leadership contributions.

Bob is a co-founder and a past President of the CAPS Vancouver & BC Chapter and served as 2012 President of the CAPS Edmonton Chapter.

He is a member of the NSA-Arizona Chapter and an active leader in the National Speakers Association, a charter member of the Canadian Association of Professional Speakers, as well as the Global Speakers Federation (GSF). He retired (December 2013) as a Trustee from the CAPS Foundation. He is currently the CAPS GSF Ambassador.

In 1998, Toastmasters International recognized Bob "…for his professionalism and outstanding achievements in public speaking". That August in Palm Desert, California Bob became the 48th speaker in the world to be awarded this prestigious professional level honor as an Accredited Speaker. He has been inducted into their Hall of Fame on numerous occasions for his leadership contributions.

Bob has been honoured by the United Nations Association of BC (1993) and received the CANADA 125 award (1992) for his ongoing leadership contributions to the community. In 1998, Bob joined 3 other men to sail a 65-foot gaff rigged schooner from Honolulu, Hawaii to Kobe, Japan, barely surviving a 'baby' typhoon en-route.

In November 2011 Bob was awarded the Spirit of CAPS at their annual convention, becoming the 11th speaker to earn this prestigious CAPS National award. Visit: www.ideaman.net/SoC.htm

Bob loves to travel and his speaking and writing have allowed him to visit 69 countries so far. Perhaps your organization would like to bring Bob in to share a few ideas with your leaders and teams around the globe. Contact him at: **www.ideaman.net**

Bob presenting at the AFCP conference in Paris, France

Visit: **www.HaveMouthWillTravel.com** for more information

Copyright and license notes

Create YOUR Future! (updated 3rd edition)
Idea-rich innovative leadership

Bob 'Idea Man' Hooey, Accredited Speaker

Cover design: **Wendy** (www.fiverr.com/craftarc)
Photos of Bob: **Dov Friedman**,
www.photographybyDov.com
Photos of Bob: **Frédéric Bélot,**
www.fredericbelot.fr/fr
Editorial/design: **Irene Gaudet**,
www.vitrakcreative.com

ISBN: 9781998014187
Printed in Canada & United States 10 9 8 7 6 5 4 3 2 1
Success Publications – a division of Creativity Corner Inc.
Box 10, Egremont, AB T0A 0Z0
www.successpublications.ca

Acknowledgements, credits, and disclaimers

As with each of my books, a very special dedication of this piece of myself, to the two people who meant the most to me, my folks **Ron and Marge Hooey**. Sadly, both my parents left this earthly realm in 1999. I still miss our time together and your encouragement and love.

תודה
Dankie Gracias
Спасибо Merci شكرا Takk
Köszönjük Terima kasih
Grazie Dziękujemy Dėkojame
Ďakujeme Vielen Dank Paldies
Kiitos Täname teid 谢谢
Thank You Tak
感谢您 Obrigado Teşekkür Ederiz
Σας Ευχαριστούμ 감사합니다
Bedankt ขอบคุณ
Děkujeme vám
ありがとうございます
Tack

I was blessed with the two of you in my life.

To my inspiring wife and professional proof reader and publications coach, **Irene Gaudet**, who loves, encourages, and supports me in my quest to continue sharing my **Ideas At Work!** across the world. Thank you seems so inadequate for your timely work in helping make my writing and my client service better! I love the time we spend together!

My thanks to the many people who have encouraged me in my growth as a leader, speaker, and engaging trainer in each area of expertise including 'Create Your Future'.

To my colleagues and friends in the National Speakers Association (NSA), the Canadian Association of Professional Speakers (CAPS), and the Global Speakers Federation (GSF) who continually challenge me to strive for success and increased excellence.

(Bob pictured seeing if the shoe fits in Holland)

To my great audiences, leaders, students, coaching clients, and readers across the globe who share their experiences and enjoyment of my work. Your positive and supportive feedback encourages me to keep working on additional programs and success publications like this updated version. My experience with you creates the foundation for additional real-life experiences I can take from the stage to the page, the classroom to the boardroom.

My thanks to a select few friends for your ongoing support and 'constructive' abuse. You know who you are. ☺

Disclaimer

We have not attempted to cite all the authorities and sources consulted in the preparation of this book. Inspiration was drawn from many sources, in this updated creation of **'Create Your Future.'**

This book is written and designed to provide information on more effective use of your time, as a life and leadership enhancement guide. It is sold with the 'explicit' understanding that the publisher and/or the author are not engaged in rendering legal, accounting, or other professional services. If legal or other expert assistance is required, the services of a competent professional in your geographic area should be sought. Its primary purpose is to complement, amplify, and supplement other books and reference materials already available. You are encouraged to search out and study all the available material, learn as much as possible, and tailor the information to your individual needs. This will help to enhance your success in being a more effective sales person, leader or professional.

Every effort has been made to make this book as complete and as accurate as possible within the scope of its focus. However, there may be mistakes, both typographical and in content or attribution. Graphics are royalty free or under license. Care has been taken to trace ownership of copyright material contained in this volume.

The publisher will gladly receive information that will allow him to rectify any reference or credit line in subsequent editions. This book should be used only as a general guide and not as the ultimate source of information. Furthermore, this book contains information that is current only up to the date of publication.

The purpose of **'Create Your Future'** is to educate and entertain; perhaps to inform and to inspire. It is certainly to challenge its readers to learn and apply its secrets and tips, to challenge them to enhance their skills and leverage their time to create more productive outcomes.

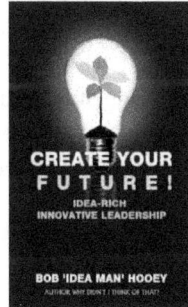

CREATE YOUR FUTURE!

IDEA-RICH
INNOVATIVE LEADERSHIP

BOB 'IDEA MAN' HOOEY
AUTHOR, WHY DIDN'T I THINK OF THAT?

The author and publisher shall have neither liability nor responsibility to any person or entity with respect to any loss or damage caused, or alleged to have been caused, directly or indirectly, by the information contained in this book.

Bob's B.E.S.T. publications

Bob is a prolific author who has been capturing and sharing his wisdom and experience in print and electronic formats for the past fifteen plus years. In addition to the following publications, several of them best sellers, he has written for consumer, corporate, professional associations, trade, and on-line publications. He has been engaged to write and assist on publications by other best-selling writers and successful companies. His publications are listed to give you an idea of the scope and topics he writes about.

Bob's **B**usiness **E**nhancement **S**uccess **T**ools.
Leadership, business, and career development series

- **Running TOO Fast** (8th edition 2022)
- **Legacy of Leadership** (6th edition 2024)
- **Make ME Feel Special!** (6th edition 2022)
- **Why Didn't I 'THINK' of That?** (5th edition 2022)
- **Speaking for Success!** (10th edition 2023)
- **Think Beyond the FIRST Sale** (3rd edition 2022)
- **Prepare Yourself to Win!** (3rd edition 2017)

Bob's Mini-book success series
- **The Courage to Lead!** (4th edition 2024)
- **Creative Conflict** (3rd edition 2024)
- **Get to YES!** (4th edition 2023)
- **THINK Before You Ink!** (3rd edition 2017)
- **Running to Win!** (3rd edition 2017)
- **Generate More Sales** (4th edition 2023)
- **Unleash your Business Potential** (3rd edition 2017)
- **Learn to Listen** (2nd edition 2017)
- **Create Your Future!** (3rd edition 2024)
- Thanks Mom!
- Dad, You're Still My Hero!

Bob's Pocket Wisdom series
- Pocket Wisdom for Selling Professionals
- Pocket Wisdom for Speakers
- Pocket Wisdom for Innovators
- Pocket Wisdom for Leaders – Power of One!
- Pocket Wisdom for Business Builders
- Additional PW books are coming in 2024

Co-authored books created by Bob
- Quantum Success – 3 volume series (2006)
- In The Company of Leaders (3rd Edition 2014)
- Foundational Success (2nd Edition 2013)

Visit: www.SuccessPublications.ca for more information on Bob's publications and other success resources.

What they say about Bob 'Idea Man' Hooey

As I travel across North America, and more recently around the globe, sharing my Ideas At Work!, I am fortunate to get feedback and comments from my audiences and colleagues. These comments come from people who have been touched, challenged, or simply enjoyed themselves in one of my sessions.

I'd love to come and share some ideas with your organization and teams.

"I've known Bob for several years and follow his activities in business with interest. I originally met Bob when he spoke for a Rotary Leadership Institute and got to know him better when he came to Vladivostok, Russia to speak to our leadership. When you spoke, I thought you were one of us because you talked about our challenges just like yours. You could understand the others, which makes you a great speaker!" **Andrey Konyushok**, Rotary International District 2225 Governor 2012-2013, far eastern Russia

"We greatly appreciate the energy and effort you put into researching and adapting your keynote to make it more meaningful to our member councils. Early feedback from our delegates indicates that this year's convention was one of our most successful events yet, and we thank you for your contribution to this success." **Larry Goodhope**, Executive Director Alberta Association of Municipal Districts and Counties

"I still get comments from people about your presentation. Only a few speakers have left an impression that lasts that long. You hit a spot with the tourism people." **Janet Bell**, Yukon Economic Forums

"Thank you, Bob, it is always a pleasure to see a true professional at work. You have made the name 'Speaker' stand out as a truism - someone who encourages people to examine their lives and make adjustments. The personal stories you shared with your audience made such a great impression on everyone. The comments indicated you hit people right where it is important - in their hearts. Each of those in your audience took away a new feeling of personal success and encouragement." **Sherry Knight**, Dimension Eleven Human Resources and Communications

"Bob is one of those rare individuals who knows how to tackle obstacles in life to reach his dreams. He takes each as a learning experience and stretches for more. His compassion and genuine interest in others make him an exceptional coach." **Cindy Kindret**, Training Manager, Silk FM Radio

"Without doubt, I have gained immeasurable self-assurance. Bob, your patience and your encouragement has been much appreciated. I strongly recommend your course to anyone looking for self-improvement and professional development." **Jeannie Mura**, Human Resources Chevron Canada

"I am pleased to recommend Bob 'Idea Man' Hooey to any organization looking for a charismatic, confident speaker and seminar leader. I have seen Bob in action on several occasions, and he is ALWAYS on! Bob has the ability to grab his audience's attention and keep it. Quite simply, if Bob is involved - your program or seminar is guaranteed to succeed." **Maurice Laving**, Coordinator Training and Development, London Drugs

Engage Bob for your leaders and their teams

"I have been so excited working with Bob Hooey, as he has given inspiration and motivation to our leadership team members. Both at the Brick Warehouse – Alberta and here at Art Van Furniture – Michigan; with his years of experience in working with business executives and his humorous and delightful packaging of his material, he makes learning with Bob a real joy. But most importantly, **anyone who encounters his material is the better for it."**

Kim Yost, CEO Art Van Furniture, former CEO The Brick

- **Motivate** your teams, your employees, and your leaders to 'productively' grow and 'profitably' succeed!

- **Protect** your conference investment - leverage your training dollars.

- **Enhance** your professional career and sell more products and services.

- **Equip** and motivate your leaders and their teams to grow and succeed, 'even' in tough times!

- **Leverage** your time to enhance your skills, equip your teams, and better serve your clients.

- **Leverage** your leadership and investment of time to leave a significant legacy!

Call today to engage best-selling author, award winning, inspirational leadership keynote speaker, leaders' success coach, and employee development trainer, Bob 'Idea Man' Hooey and his innovative, audience based, results-focused, Ideas At Work! for your next company, convention, leadership, staff, training, or association event. You'll be glad you did!

Call 1-780-736-0009 to connect with **Bob 'Idea Man' Hooey** today!

Learn more about Bob at: **www.ideaman.net** or **www.BobHooey.training**

PRO-tips: Leaders, Managers, Owners

We'd suggest this book might be a great reference and discussion guide for you and your team. Work through it and discuss where it is relevant in your specific client interaction and culture. Working to create a creative team and client centered culture will pay dividends for years to come. We've made **'Create Your Future!** available as a lower investment E-pub version. Why not get each team member their own copy of the E-pub version? If you'd like to make a bulk order, please contact me and we'll work something out, just for you.

Email: **bob@ideaman.net**
www.SuccessPublications.ca

CREATIVITY

*" Creativity has been built into everyone of us;
it's part of our design.*

*Each of us lives less of the life God intended
for us when we choose not to live out
the creative powers we possess."*
Ted Engstrom

*"Creativity is especially expressed in the ability to
make connections, to make associations, to turn
things around and express them in a new way."*
Tim Hansen

*"One of the major factors which differentiates creative
people from lesser creative people is that creative
people pay attention to their small ideas."*
Roger von Oech

"We do not yet trust the unknown powers of thought."
Ralph Waldo Emerson

*"Nothing is more dangerous than an idea,
when it's the only idea you have."*
Linus Pauling

*"There is no doubt that creativity is the most
important human resource of all. Without
creativity, there would be no progress, and we
would be forever repeating the same patterns."*
Edward de Bono